Chimayo Valley Traditions

A religious procession approaching the Santuario in Potrero ca. 1917. Photo by Jesse Nusbaum, courtesy of the Museum of New Mexico, negative number 14379.

Chimayo Valley Traditions

by

Elizabeth Kay

Ancient City Press
Santa Fe, New Mexico

 **Printed on Recycled Paper**

Contents

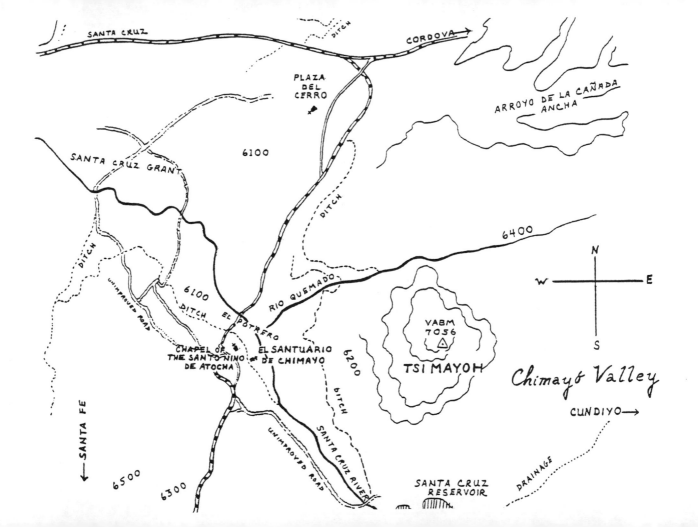

Acknowledgements

I would like to thank all the people who helped me in one way or another to write this book: to my parents, Kenneth and Phyllis Charline Kay; to Dr. Marta Weigle and Dr. Alfonso Ortiz from the University of New Mexico Departments of American Studies and Anthropology who were helpful and generous with their knowledge of Indian and Hispanic history; to Nick Abdalla, Gara Antreasian, Jane Abrams and Joe Rothrock from the University Art Department who encouraged the project; to Raymond Bal and his parents Elma and Robert Bal of Chimayo who continue to offer insight about the valley; and to Mary Powell of Ancient City Press and John Boland and Andrew Smith of the Andrew Smith Gallery for their invaluable technical assistance. Finally, this book is dedicated to the memory of Kenneth Kay, Marguerite Nolan and Freda Bockhold.

Chimayó Valley

Man dwells when he can orientate himself within and identify himself with an environment, or, in short, when he experiences the environment as meaningful. Dwelling therefore implies something more than "shelter." It implies that the spaces where life occurs are places, *in the true sense of the word. A place is a space which has a distinct character. Since ancient times the* genius loci, *or "spirit of place," has been recognized as the concrete reality man has to face and come to terms within his daily life.*

—Christian Norberg-Schulz, Genius Loci: Towards a Phenomenology of Architecture.

Of a God "in whom we live and move and have our being" we cannot say that He is in space as we are, but much rather that He is the "space" in which we are.

—Ananda K. Coomaraswamy, Traditional Art and Symbolism.

Pilgrimage...is like a vertical shaft driven into the past, disclosing deep strata of ancient symbols, potent signifiers which reinforce nationalistic sentiments.

—Victor Turner and Edith Turner, Image and Pilgrimage in Christian Culture.

Capilla del Santo Niño

Prologue: The Sanctuaries of El Potrero

ALTHOUGH NOT SO OLD OR FAMOUS as the nearby Santuario de Chimayó, the Capilla del Santo Niño de Atocha in El Potrero attracts a steady flow of visitors and pilgrims who come to venerate the Holy Child of Atocha. The inside of the *capilla* (chapel) reflects their tremendous devotion. An array of statues, crosses, flowers, paintings, candles, banners, and baby shoes decorate numerous altars and shelves.

Generations of New Mexico's Hispanic families have grown up hearing tales of the Santo Niño's nightlong errands of mercy about the countryside during which He wears out His shoes. Hence, there still exists the custom of placing an offering of baby shoes at the foot of His statue. The chapel has more modern figurines of Christ, the Virgin, the Holy child, and the saints than older churches in the area, and some visitors may find it lacks historical charm. But to the faithful who worship here, the capilla is the home of the Santo Niño de Atocha to whom they appeal in times of trouble.

The Capilla del Santo Niño and the Santuario de Chimayó were El Potrero's center for mass and feast day celebrations until the construction of the Holy Family Church in 1967 along the Santa Cruz highway. Older residents like Elma Bal, proprietor of the Potrero Trading Post, recall hearing the bells of the chapel ring on December 23, summoning the people of Chimayó to pray the novena of El Santo Niño de Atocha for nine days. On Christmas Day the chapel was decorated with candles and colored paper for High Mass. Afterwards children and adults joined in a procession through El Potrero praying for a good new year.

On New Year's Eve *luminarias* (small bonfires) of pitchwood were lit throughout the village and on top of the hill, their brightness symbolizing the death of the old year. After High Mass the Medina family who owned the Niño chapel gave a dinner for all the parishioners. The festivities often lasted all night with singing and guitar music. A piñon tree decorated with popcorn, rosehips and colorful handmade objects stood near tables laden with posole, red chile, *biscochitos* (cookies), *empanaditas* (little fried pies), and bread baked in outdoor ovens. The following morning children went from house to house receiving homemade pastries and candy from neighbors.

In the past private chapels were very common in Hispanic villages of northern New Mexico, but today the capilla in El Potrero, which is still open to the public, is something of a rarity. The chapel has always been in the Medina family since Severiano Medina built it in 1857 to honor the Holy Child of Atocha. Until their deaths in 1985, Ramon and Saranita Medina owned the chapel and ran a small store next door. A rather touching characteristic of the little store was a supply of baby shoes that Saranita gave at no charge to those who wanted to make a votive offering to El Santo Niño de Atocha.

Well into old age Ramon and Saranita continued to care for their chapel—unlocking its white wooden doors in the morning, scrubbing the linoleum floors, pruning and watering the thick juniper and lilac bushes in the tiny courtyard, and replacing votive candles as they burned out. A small metal box inside the chapel for donations helped cover their expenses.

When Saranita died in 1985 she was buried in the chapel courtyard on a rainy spring day. The rain was taken as a good omen by mourners at the funeral that her soul had been accepted into heaven. Ramon died the following July and was buried next to his wife. His brothers, few of whom live in Chimayó, have inherited the chapel, and his daughter who has moved into the family store now undertakes the chapel's upkeep. How much longer the Capilla del Santo Niño de Atocha will remain a private chapel is uncertain. Already there is talk in the community of its being purchased by the Catholic Church.

Half a century ago the Santuario de Chimayó experienced a similar transition when it ceased to be privately owned by a Potrero family and became the property of the Catholic Church. Certain changes were bound to occur: land boundaries have been more clearly defined, sidewalks and parking spaces added to accommodate visitors, gift shops opened, and a priest is generally available to visitors. While no one can predict what changes might occur if the Santo Niño chapel becomes the property of the Church, certainly the days when a kind old lady gave away shoes to pious visitors will not return.

The southern portion of the Chimayó valley where the Capilla del Santo Niño de Atocha and the Santuario de Chimayó lie has been considered sacred for centuries. The Pueblo Indians of the upper Rio Grande watershed regarded it as a shrine in pre-Hispanic times. The Spanish who settled there after the Reconquest built the Santuario de Chimayó and the Capilla del Santo Niño de Atocha more than a century later. In recent times Anglos interested in history and folk art have worked to preserve the valley and learn more about its Spanish-Indian heritage.

Over centuries three different cultures, each in its own way, have responded to the mystical lure of Chimayó. This high, remote valley is a place of myth and legend. Its shrines and chapels which continue to draw pilgrims are evidence of its special spiritual appeal to men and women of different races and beliefs.

Tsi Mayoh and Tewa Indian Beliefs

THE WINDING HIGHWAY BETWEEN THE FERTILE VALLEYS of Nambe and Chimayó passes through an arid region of gulches and eroded standstone, the colorful "badlands" of the Española Valley. Within this forbidding yet beautiful landscape is one of the highest hills in the area, called Tsi Mayoh by the Tewa Indians of San Juan Pueblo (Ortiz 1969: 10). Tsi Mayoh,[1] which is 7,056 feet high, rises above the southeast corner of the Chimayó valley known as El Potrero. Like the surrounding hills and mesas Tsi Mayoh is composed of loose pink granite and covered with a sparse growth of juniper and piñon scrub. A small cave, sacred to the Tewa, opens on its northwest face and from its peak can be seen Sandia Mountain ninety miles south, Canjilon Peak sixty miles north, Tsikomo Mountain twenty-five miles west, and the Truchas Peaks ten miles east.

Twenty million years ago violent volcanic action in what is now the southwestern United

Tsi Mayoh

States thrust up mountain ridges and created vast basin- like depressions called calderas inside cooling volcano craters. In what was to become north-central New Mexico lakes formed, fed by the Rio Grande River. These eventually dried up as the river changed course. Over the ages these dry, sedimentary lake beds were eroded into spectacular red and tan formations by wind and water that also cut canyons and river valleys in the earth. The results are visible today around the towns of Española, Chimayó, and Santa Cruz where verdant river valleys contrast with grotesquely sculpted pinnacles and mesas (Christiansen and Kottlowski 1967:38). Since prehistoric time the inhabitants of this arid land have treasured these green valleys for their rich, alluvial soil and precious water for irrigation.

A classic example is the Chimayó valley, which lies between the Rio Grande and the Sangre de Cristo mountains. Watered by two rivers and numerous springs in the surrounding cliffs, Chimayó is about two miles long and a quarter-mile wide at the bottom, widening to more than a mile where its northern end stops abruptly at a sheer cliff. At 6,100 feet above sea level Chimayó lies high in the Upper Sonoran Zone which begins above 4,500 feet and covers some three- fourths of the state. The Zone is dry at lower elevations and supports only scant vegetation, but higher up, as at Chimayó, rain and run-off water nurture piñon, juniper, sage brush, and some trees (Beck 1962:10). Steep rounded hills covered with dry scrub rise two to nine hundred feet north and west of the valley. Those on the west slope gradually to the Rio Grande five hundred feet below and the eastern ones climb toward the 13,000-foot Truchas Peaks.

The rivers that water the Chimayó valley are the Rio Quemado, rising in the Truchas Peaks, and the larger Santa Cruz which flows from a small reservoir southeast of the valley. The Rio

Quemado eventually joins the Santa Cruz which ultimately empties into the Rio Grande near Española ten miles west. Both rivers supply water to an intricate system of irrigation ditches in the eastern and western parts of the valley. Ditches north of the Santa Cruz are fed by springs in the cliffs that flow down arroyos and gullies bearing old Spanish names such as Arroyo de la Cuesta de los Vaqueros (Cowboy Hill Stream), Arroyo de la Cueva (Cave Stream), and Arroyo de la Morada.

Chimayo's elevation gives it a shorter growing season than New Mexico's average of 148 to 216 days, but fertile soil and bountiful water compensate. Livestock, chile, fruit, beans, wheat, and corn all flourish, the chile and fruit of Chimayó being considered particularly fine.

The Pueblo Indians who settled along the Rio Grande river and its tributaries between A.D. 1100 and 1400 were probably the first people to view the fertile area known as Chimayó as sacred. Like other Pueblo tribes of the Rio Grande region, the Tewa Indians of San Juan Pueblo (originally called Ohke) define the world they live in by setting boundaries to it and giving order to everything within it (Ortiz 1979:294). Mountains, hills, or lakes aligned with the cardinal directions are sacred boundary markers believed to be inhabited by deities who protect the villages (Ortiz 1969:10; Parsons 1939:149).

For that and other reasons these high places are considered to be holy. Moisture was vital to survival in the arid land of the Pueblos and the mountain tops, often cloud-covered and struck by lightning, seemed obvious sources of wind, clouds, and rain. Like many other tribes the Tewa have hundreds of songs and stories about sacred mountains that protect them from harm and are a powerful source of psychological comfort. Some mountains were so sacred that no one could walk on them except members of a particular tribe and then only at certain times of the

San Juan Pueblo

year. For some tribes fighting was forbidden on the sacred mountain, even when meeting an enemy there (Curtis 1926:12).

Among tribal traditions is a complex system of shrines which the Tewa of the Rio Grande Valley constructed in the cardinal directions from inside their pueblos to the mesas, hills, and mountains beyond. Each direction is associated with a particular color: blue/green to the north, yellow to the west, red to the south, and white to the east. The directional circuit from shrine to shrine begins in the north and moves west, south, and east.

The shrines that form the boundaries of the Tewa world for San Juan Pueblo are four mountains: Canjilon Peak to the north, Tsikomo Mountain in the west, Sandia Crest in the south, and Truchas Peak in the east. Being closest to the pueblo, Tsikomo is the most important shrine in San Juan rituals just as Lake Peak in the Truchas Mountains is most important to pueblos on the east side of the Rio Grande (Ortiz 1969:141). On top of each mountain stands a shrine known as an earth navel and built of stones loosely arranged in a keyhole shape, its opening facing the village. Earth navels are believed to generate blessings and direct them back toward the mother earth navel in the sacred center of the pueblo, thus keeping "everything good and desirable" within the Tewa world (Ortiz 1969:22).

In the Pueblo world shrines can take many forms: a boulder shelter, a rocky ledge, a cave, or a cairn of stones. Like sacred lakes, ponds, and earth navels, shrines are points at which one can communicate with ancestral spirits, for it is believed that after death the soul goes immediately to one of the four directional shrines (Ortiz 1969:52).

Four flat-topped hills nearer the pueblo comprise a second group of formations sacred to the Tewa. The northern hill called Tema Yoh rises just above the Spanish village of La Madera. A few miles to the southwest stands Toma Yoh; Yun Yoh lies to the south between San Ildefonso and Santa Clara, and off in the east is Tsi Mayoh. These are dark, forbidding hills, each with a cave or tunnel believed to be the entrance to the underworld. They are dangerous places for anyone except the priests, for they are inhabited by the Towa é or "little people" (Ortiz 1969:19).

In a larger sense Tsi Mayoh and the three other sacred hills are important on a symbolic level. Space is categorized by gender, the women's domain being the village, the men's the mountains. The village domain took in cultivated fields, river bottom lands, and nearby, low hills where women and children gathered wild plants and caught small game. The far-off mountain regions, homes of the deities and larger game, could only be entered by initiated men and boys. Tsi Mayoh and its three companion, sacred hills assume a special symbolic importance because they constitute a mediation area which both sexes can visit although men are in charge of it and women usually go only in the company of men.

The hills are a mediating region in another sense as well. The caves and fissures in them provide entry into the underworld where the androgynous Towa é act as mediators between the metaphorical, mythical time of emergence from below earth to the actual, historical one of earth-surface existence. "Spatially, socially, sexually, spiritually, and even in subsistence terms," the middle space of the four sacred hills between village lands and mountains is an ambivalent, mediating area (Ortiz 1969:284).

It was a practice of the Rio Grande Pueblo people to make midsummer pilgrimages to their sacred hills and mountains to clean shrines, sweep the trails to them, and pray for rain. They

Tsi Komo Mountain

regarded the shrines as springs from which the rain flowed and believed that accumulated debris would block the flow (Curtis 1926:12). Prayer meal or loose feathers would be sprinkled on the shrines to send messages to the gods. On these pilgrimages the villagers could not eat, gather, or kill anything they passed (Parsons 1939:178).

The Towa é who guard the sacred hills are one of the Pueblo universals. Variously referred to as the war spirits, the little war gods, the War Brothers, or Twins, they are the founders, inventors, and culture heroes frequently mentioned in Pueblo myth and legend (Parsons 1939:936). Begotten by the Sun or Water or, as in the Tewa origin myth, existing with the people at the time of Emergence, the Twins are credited with such things as producing order by finding the cardinal directions, creating mountains and valleys, leading the people in migrations, introducing curing societies, and saving the people from monsters or dangerous persons (Parsons 1939:211). But the Twins are tricky, unreliable spirits even when benign. Being precisely neither male or female, child or adult, the Twins personify duality, a concept suggesting that as divine beings they embody attributes of both sexes and thus have supernatural power (Eliade 1958:421).

The Towa é of the Tewa figure more often in myth than in folktales. According to the origin myth, at the time of the emergence the Tewa were living under a sacred lake to the north, and among them were the Towa é, six sets of brothers who created order by identifying the sacred mountains of the four directions. They also created the sacred hills by flinging mud to the north, west, south and east. After defining the boundaries of the Tewa world and assisting the people to the surface of the earth, the Towa é retreated to the hills and mountains where they remained, mysterious and undefined, guarding the Tewa pueblos from their high vantage points.

Tsi Mayoh was sacred to the Tewa, but how they used the hill can only be surmised. Perhaps a priest climbed it each dawn to worship the sun (Harrington 1916:81). However, according to Ortiz, the sacred hill to the south was the one most important to the pueblo's religious beliefs and rituals. Even so, Tsi Mayoh's location in the east must have given it great spiritual significance because of the association with the rising sun, the source of all life to the Tewa and the primary fertilizing agent in nature (Ortiz 1969:154).

Stories collected in the twentieth century from Indian narrators suggest that a pueblo once stood where the Santuario de Chimayó now stands. Nearby was a pool from which the Indians took mud and earth in order to cure sickness:

The Indians say that Chimayó used to be a Tewa Indian pueblo, then called *Tsimajo'onwi (onwi* 'pueblo'). This pueblo was situated where the church now is, the informants stated. The church is on the south side of the creek. Where the church now is there used to be a pool, they say, called *Tsimajopokwi (pokwi* 'pool'...). The earth or mud of this pool has healing properties... (Harrington 1916:342).

Within this century comes evidence that the pit of healing earth used to contain more moisture than it does today. In her book about the famous potter from San Ildefonso, María Martínez, Alice Marriott describes the child's first pilgrimage to the shrine at Chimayó:

There was darkness behind the door—darkness and a sense of depth. Mother drew Maria towards

Sacred Cave on Tsi Mayoh

15

it. The child smelled an earthen dampness, like the darkness of the storeroom at home, and it surprised her. Most churches smelled of dry dust, not wet (Marriott 1948:37).

Other narrators say that when the Twins killed a Giant inhabiting a hill near Tsi Mayoh, fire burst out in several places, drying the pool and leaving behind only healing mud (Borhegyi 1956:8). According to one version:

In a cave on the north side of Tú yo, a precipitous basaltic hill north of San Ildefonso, lived the giant Tsi-mayó (obsidian chief). He had a huge oven on the summit beside the trail. He devoured people. One step carried him to San Ildefonso, three steps to Santa Clara, and with an armful of children he would return to roast them in his oven. One day the Towa é were playing near the hill. They had come down from Sipófene for the purpose of killing the monster. When the giant went to San Ildefonso, they followed him. He tried to catch them, but they eluded him. Finally they drove him to Shúma (the volcanic mesa south of the village at the beginning of the Rio Grande gorge). There they destroyed him, and smoke belched forth from Shúma, from Tsimayó (Chimayó mountain northeast of the village), from a large cave in a northern mountain, and the cave in Tú yo (Curtis 1926:172).

This legend supports the frequently cited belief that within the time of the Tewa the basaltic hills near San Ildefonso, Santa Clara, and San Juan were volcanically active (Borhegyi 1956:8; Harrington 1916:341-343).

These stories can be considered against certain facts: that archaeological ruins exist near the

Santuario de Chimayó and that the area was apparently inhabited from 1100 A.D. to 1400 A.D. continuously, although no Indians appear to have been living in the valley when the Spanish arrived (Borhegyi 1956:8). As for the legendary pool, of which no evidence survives, several pools can be found not far off from the present day Santuario, and hot mineral springs are common in the neighboring Jemez Mountains and near the hill at Ojo Caliente.

There is some evidence for Indian use of mud with curative power. Certain Southwest tribes used spring water for medicine, and at Laguna Pueblo clay balls found on the riverbank were considered to have healing properties (Parsons 1939:416). In Oraibi the Hopi rubbed damp clay on their bodies in a war ritual. Borhegyi notes that geophagy (eating earth) was practiced by Zunis, Hopis, and Navajos. María Martínez was instructed by her mother to drink the sacred earth from Chimayó mixed with water:

"You will have to mix it in water and drink it before breakfast every morning for the next four days," her mother answered. "This is good earth. The Indians knew about it and how to use it a long time ago. Then the padres came and learned about its power, and the Santo Niño came and told them what to do, so they built the church here. Everybody knows that the earth is good. It makes everyone well who drinks it, for the rest of his life" (Marriott 1948:37).

It is therefore not unlikely that the Pueblo people were using Chimayó mud for its therapeutic value at the time the Spanish arrived. This might even help explain how the Spanish settlers came to associate the "blessed" earth at Chimayó with a Catholic shrine in Latin America whose soil was also supposed to work miracles.

Plaza del Cerro

The Spanish Settle Chimayo

SHORTLY AFTER THE PUEBLO REVOLT (1680-1692), several groups of Spanish colonists settled in the northwestern section of the fertile Chimayó valley. Records of land deeds and disputes over lands in Chimayó date back to 1714 and settlement may have begun as many as two decades earlier. The first clear references to the *paraje de Tzimayo* appear in the 1740s, and it is likely that the Plaza del Cerro was built at this time (Larcombe 1983:172).

The Plaza del Cerro is a square enclosed by contiguous adobe buildings with only three entrance-ways, just wide enough to admit animals and people on foot and thus easily defensible. On the south side of the plaza stands a *torreón* or defensive watch tower. The *acequia madre*, or main irrigation ditch, runs through the plaza. To the west is a small chapel called the Oratorio de San Buenaventura (Larcombe 1983:172). At the southern end of the valley, below the hill Tsi Mayoh, lies a separate settlement called El Potrero, a name that suggests it was the pastureland of the community in earlier centuries (Borhegyi 1956:9).

In 1754 twelve heads of families from Santa Cruz and Chimayó petitioned the Capitan-General of the province for a tract of public, national farm land on the plateau between the Rio Truchas and the Rio Quemaeo for the purpose of settlement and cultivation. Such outposts to the east were regarded as desirable buffers between the marauding Indians of the plains and the Spanish colonists along the Rio Grande (Atkins 1978:iii).

Like other colonists of northern New Mexico, those who settled Chimayó were true *paisanos* who lived off the land and close to it. A hymn of the region reflects this:

De la tierra fui formado,	From the earth I was made,
La tierra me a de comer;	And the earth shall eat me,
La tierra me a sustantado,	The earth has sustained me,
Y al fin yo tierra ha de ser.	And at last earth I shall be also.
	(Henderson 1937:103).

The *españoles* were hard working, independent farmers and artisans whose occupations included weaving, day labor and stock raising (Jones 1978:147). They had not come to New Mexico for religious freedom or civil liberties but because there was a chance of receiving the title *hidalgo* (nobleman) if they stayed. Frequently they were granted land, building lots, subsidies, and farming implements for their new life on the frontier.

Life was frugal and hardship common to the early settlers. Produce was raised on small plots

Farmer in El Potrero

watered by irrigation ditches. Goats and sheep provided milk, cheese, wool, and meat. From native plants dyes and soaps were obtained. Droughts, hailstorms and frost often threatened crops and wild animals were a menace to both crops and stock.

Nomadic Indians raided the communities throughout the seventeenth and eighteenth centuries, costing settlers both lives and hard-won provisions. In 1748 the villagers of Córdova fled to Chimayó from one such attack. While women and children remained in Chimayó, the men returned to Córdova to cultivate fields while a sentry posted on the hill watched for Indians. Such constant threats to property and lives drew the communities close together physically and socially (Brown 1978:12).

In early years the colonists were not allowed to move throughout the province at their own discretion. Spanish officials tried to maintain control over the northern provinces by requiring any who wished to leave a community to petition for and obtain an official government permit specifying who they were, where they were going, for what purpose, and how long they intended to be gone (Jones 1978:147). This immobility increased the sense of isolation of these early New Mexicans. People who did travel frequently, such as caravan mule packers, gypsies, and the *comancheros* who traded with the Comanches, were regarded with awe by the sedentary villagers.

Isolated hundreds of miles from the larger settlements of El Paso del Norte, Chihuahua, Tucson, San Antonio de Bixar, and Alto California, the Spanish settlements depended for supplies on mule trains that came up from Mexico every few years. In the late summer caravans from Chimayó and other settlements traveled south to fairs in Chihuahua, sometimes going as far as Mexico City, trips that could take as long as six months (Brown 1978:86; Simmons 1983b:85-86). Often entire families went because it was safer than leaving members at home under the threat of Apache and Navaho raids. Such a trip might be made only once in a lifetime and was a festive occasion during which stories and songs were exchanged, shrines visited, foods, spices, and material items replenished, and sometimes new husbands or wives acquired in Mexico.

During the eighteenth century agricultural communities like Chimayó developed as hard-working, self-defending, and self-sufficient units. Lacking outside contact and goods the settlers used natural resources and native remedies for their needs, such as herbs, folk remedies, and even Indian medicine. To transport goods New Mexicans built *carretas*. They refined traditional techniques such as making adobe bricks from mud and straw for building materials. Having little paper they used buffalo hides to paint on (Jones 1978:149).

The Spanish colonists were devout Catholics with a deep reverence for the tangible side of Catholicism: its symbols, images and rituals. Prayer entered into virtually every activity or under-taking from cooking to agriculture (Jaramillo 1941:26). Every month included religious obser-vances, and some had as many as seven holy days, which were often linked to seasonal changes. Planting could not occur in the spring until after Holy Week and farmers watched the phases of the sun and moon closely, planting only when they judged moisture would be most likely. In the spring villagers carried a carved *santo* of San Isidro, patron saint of farmers, through the fields to bless the crops, encourage fertility, and grant a bounteous harvest in the fall (Brown 1978:186; Briggs 1983). On San Juan day (June 24) it was believed the waters in streams were holy, for on that day St. John had baptized Jesus in the River Jordan and blessed the waters (Jaramillo 1941:85).

Santa Cruz Church ca. 1870

Before a new settlement was complete a church had to be built and furnished with holy representations of Christ, the Virgin Mary and the Saints—images made by local craftsmen (*santeros*) or brought from Mexico by the caravans. Light was a symbol used for Jesus and the Virgin in New Mexico and to maximize the rays of the rising sun, transverse clerestory windows, unique to New Mexico, were built above the roof that covered the rest of the church. Through them sunlight flooded onto images and statues at the nave of the church, conveying a sense of Presence to the faithful and likely affecting the Indians being converted to Christianity. The entrance of the church generally faced east to receive the light of the rising sun although chapels that faced south had the benefit of winter light (Kubler 1940:67).

Despite the importance of religion in the lives of the colonists there were never enough priests to cover the vast frontier and some villages were visited no more than once a year by the local priest stationed at a pueblo. In 1706 the inhabitants of Chimayó were ministered by a priest from San Juan Pueblo, but in 1751 the settlement of San Buenaventura de Chimayó, as it was called, fell under the jurisdiction of Santa Cruz de la Cañada, the administrative center for the area north of Santa Fe throughout the Spanish and early Mexican periods.

In the latter half of the eighteenth century there were seldom ecclesiastics to minister in times of sickness and death or to celebrate important religious observances and these duties were performed by the Penitente Brotherhood that developed in the Santa Cruz area sometime between ca. 1790 and 1833 (Weigle 1976:19-51; Steele and Rivera 1985:3-11). The Penitente Brotherhood, commonly known as *Los Hermanos Penitentes* or *Los Hermanos*, provided lay religious and welfare services for the villages during the so-called Secular Period (ca.1790-1850) when the Franciscans were replaced by secular priests supported by parishoners and not by the crown. Filling the com-

Death Cart

munity's need for spiritual guidance in times of death or, most importantly, during Lenten and Holy Week rituals, the Brotherhood was a strong cultural force, preserving language, lore, customs, and faith. Through prayer and bodily penance sin was expiated in this unique folk religion that in later years would acquire both judicial and political influence (Weigle 1970:3).

Between 1780 and 1781 there arose a desperate need for priests during a devastating outbreak of smallpox. Plagues of various types were common in every decade of the eighteenth century but none was as constant and virulent as smallpox. Inoculation had been developed in Europe in the early eighteenth century but it is doubtful if it was used in New Mexico during the colonial era. Medical practice was rudimentary; settlers depended on the garrison surgeon, if one were in the vicinity, or on priests who often performed phlebotomy or bleeding. For the most part the settlers resorted to a wide variety of herbs, local remedies and Indian treatments (Simmons 1966:320).

The Great Smallpox Epidemic of 1780-81 was the worst ever to sweep across New Mexico and towns along the Rio Grande recorded many deaths from the disease. Albuquerque, San Felipe, Santa Fe, Santa Cruz, and Pecos were hard hit and pueblos as far northwest as Zuni and Hopi were also affected. The enormous death toll placed a great strain on both Indians and Spanish. The loss of so many young men and women drained the labor force of the communities and the psychological effects of the loss may have played a part in the new cult that was soon to appear in Chimayó. There is ample evidence that Spanish women rapidly assumed many of the basic beliefs of the Indians through contact with their Indian servants. Possibly one means of coping with the smallpox epidemic was a sudden faith in Indian remedies such as the belief that the dirt from below the hill Tsi Mayoh had medicinal powers.

Retablo of Our Lady of Sorrows, after the
santero Molleno

28

Chimayo's El Santuario de Esquipulas

THE ADOBE CATHOLIC CHAPEL AT CHIMAYÓ, El Santuario de Esquípulas,[2] owes its name, indeed its existence, and to some extent its reputation as a shrine with miraculous healing powers to a religious cult in faraway Guatemala, two thousand miles to the south. How this came about remains something of a mystery. To clarify it as much as possible a digression is in order.

By the start of the nineteenth century the town of Esquípulas in southeastern Guatemala had for two centuries been the site of a shrine visited by thousands of pilgrims annually in search of cures and blessings. The shrine was venerated for two features: a crucifix known as the Black Christ, or Nuestro Señor de Esquípulas, and the earth around the shrine which was believed to have miraculous curative powers.

The origin of the town can be traced back to the sixteenth-century Spanish Conquest of the Mayan Indians. Spanish chronicles record that in 1524 a Chorti Indian chief named Esquípulas surrendered his people without resistance to the invading Spaniards in order to prevent bloodshed. When the Chorti Indians were resettled in a new town established by the Spanish between 1560 and 1570 it was named Santiago de Esquípulas in honor of the peaceable chief. Located on an ancient trade and pilgrimage route to the Mayan ceremonial center of Copán in southeastern Honduras, the new town attracted many Mayan Indians dislocated from Copán when the Spanish conquered it in 1530. Eventually it achieved importance as a population, trade, and religious center formerly held by Copán.

Pre-Columbian Indians had long made pilgrimages to the area around Esquípulas to drink from its sulfur springs and to eat the earth, both regarded as having medicinal value. Geophagy (earth-eating) was common in Central America and Mexico. The Spanish observed early that the Aztecs ate thick layered cakes made of a slimy substance collected from the surface of Lake Texcoco, mixed with sand and earth, and dried in the sun (Borhegyi 1954:393).

Aztecs, like Mayans and other Indians, also made regular pilgrimages to sites such as Esquípulas to propitiate the deities with gifts and sacrifices. After the Conquest, Spanish priests realized that linking pagan rites to Christian beliefs would help them convert the Indians to Catholicism, a method of incorporation referred to colloquially as "baptizing the customs" (Turner 1978:33). Such linkings eventually resulted in Mexican Catholic shrines like those of Guadalupe, Ocotlán, Chalma, and Ísamal, all standing on ground long considered sacred by pre-Columbian Indians.

The Guatemalan town of Esquípulas is a typical example. In 1578 Catholic priests built a chapel near the sulfur springs there and the Christianized Indians of the locality collected fifty ounces of silver to buy a crucifix for it. Carved from dark brown balsam and orange wood, the

Esquípulas Cathedral

31

crucifix, called the Black Christ, or El Cristo Negro de Esquípulas, soon became credited with the healing powers originally attributed to the hot springs and the earth (Fergusson 1937:48-61).

How the cult of Esquípulas came to Chimayó or who brought it there is unknown. What is known is that the baptismal records of Santa Cruz parish show that in 1805 an infant from the village of El Potrero was christened with the name of Juan de Esquípulas, the first appearance ever of the name in local baptismal records. The infant was the nephew of a devout prominent citizen named Bernardo Abeyta,[3] who eight years later, in 1813, had his own son christened Tomas de Esquípulas.

Also in 1813, speaking for the nineteen or so families in El Potrero, Abeyta wrote a letter to Fray Sebastián de Alvarez of Santa Cruz parish asking permission to build a chapel to honor and venerate "with worthy worship, Our Lord and Redeemer, in His Advocation of Esquípulas." Written in early November of 1813, the letter was on good paper, a scarce commodity in colonial New Mexico. Generally when someone received a letter the writing was erased after reading and an answer written on top. Sometimes there would be as many as four writings on the same sheet. Abeyta's writing was the first on its paper, and the letter mentioned that the crucifix of Esquípulas had been worshiped for the past three years (since 1810) in the *hermita* (shelter) attached to his house and built at his own expense.

How Bernardo Abeyta learned of the distant cult of Esquípulas is a matter of conjecture. Judging by the accuracy of his spelling of the Mayan name and the iconographic similarities between the Black Christ and the crucifix carved for the Santuario de Chimayó, it seems certain that someone from the Chimayó area had seen or otherwise acquired firsthand knowledge of

Black Christ of Esquípulas

33

El Posito

the Guatemalan shrine or one of its Mexican offshoots. This is not as improbable as it may sound, in spite of the two thousand miles between northern New Mexico and Guatemala. The Viceroyalty of New Spain was tied together by a vast network of trails and roads over which passed a great volume of foot traffic as well as pack trains and cart caravans (Simmons 1983a:325; 1983b). Some merchant or traveler from Chimayó might have made the journey or perhaps one of the summer caravans to Mexico brought back a detailed description of the Black Christ and His connection with healing earth. However it happened, the cult of Esquípulas came to Chimayó and took root there at least in part because of the healing powers long attributed by Pueblo Indians to the earth near El Potrero (Borhegyi 1954:397).

Legend says that Bernardo Abeyta's *hermita* covered a hole from which came a blessed dirt that cured all ailments. It also housed a crucifix called Nuestro Señor de Esquípulas, which had been found under miraculous circumstances. In February of 1814 the residents of Potrero were given permission to build their chapel at this site by the Reverend Father Francisco de Otocio, the pastor in charge of all the missions in New Mexico. The chapel, built with adobe, was ninety feet in length and thirty feet in width, with walls three feet thick. Pinewood was used for roof beams. The choir loft and the church itself was of the continuous nave type. Its entrance faced the southwest to take advantage of the winter sunlight and within the roof a clerestory window was built.

Connected to the sacristy's northeast wall lay the room said to have originally been Abeyta's *hermita* containing *El Posito*, the hole or sacred well from which came the health-giving earth. This small room with one small window on its northeast wall was entered through a narrow doorway no more than five feet high. The floor was slightly below ground level and dipped toward the central hole which today measures approximately sixteen inches in diameter and six inches in depth.

The church originally had no benches but was lavishly decorated with *reredos*, *retablos*, and *bultos*[4] by local *santeros* (saint carvers). It is likely that the *reredos* and *bultos* presently in the Santuario were crafted between 1820 and 1850.[5] The appearance of the chapel's interior probably has not changed much since the mid-1800s, despite Bishop Lamy's well-known disapproval of the use of *santos* in the chapels (Borhegyi 1956:15).

The cult of Esquípulas spread to many other villages in northern New Mexico, including Ranchos de Taos. One of the side altars in the transept of the church of San Francisco there was devoted to Him. As for the belief in *tierra bendita* (blessed earth), only one other Catholic chapel seems to have made such a claim. In the Chapel of Our Lady of Talpa, also near Taos, there was a Spanish belief in the healing powers of the earth. However, no evidence has been found to indicate pre-Hispanic use of the earth at this site (Wroth 1979:30). This chapel was used by Penitentes in the area, suggesting influences from some of the beliefs from the Chimayó-Santa Cruz area.

Bernardo Abeyta (1771-1856) was not only instrumental in introducing the new cult of Esquípulas to Chimayó; he was also a leader in the Penitente Brotherhood that was rapidly developing in the area. The Brotherhood was not an institutionalized regional organization during the early 1800s; individuals offered leadership within their particular communities and were referred to as *Hermanos Mayores*, or Elder Brothers. Abeyta served as Hermano Mayor in the Chimayó area, and his name appears in various important Penitente documents from the nineteenth century. For example, an 1860 Constitution for "The Brotherhood of Our Father Jesus" derives "from the Rule given by the *Hermano Mayor* (Elder Brother) of the Brotherhood of Penance, the deceased Bernardo Abeyta" (Darley 1893:14). Elsewhere in these documents attributed to Abeyta's authoritative influence is mention of the *santa tierra*, or holy ground, which the novice is ordered to kiss (Steele and Rivera 1985:17).

The problem of Penitente origins has never been fully resolved and it has been suggested that the same traveler from Chimayó who know about the Esquípulas cult in Guatemala also knew about Sevillian-like penitential confraternities. Possibly Abeyta knew of such confraternities himself, for upon receiving permission to build the chapel it is said he made a trip to Mexico to purchase ornaments for it. This story, as well as the legend that he was practicing Penitente penances when he discovered the miraculous crucifix, suggest that he "could have been instrumental in establishing a penitential confraternity, the idea for which might easily have diffused from the pilgrimage center he helped found" (Weigle 1976:49-50). In any case, Bernardo Abeyta was influential in nineteenth-century New Mexican ecclesiastical history, and when he died in 1856 Bishop Lamy granted special permission for his burial in the Chapel of Our Lord of Esquípulas.

Santuario de Chimayó ca. 1900

Legends of the Miraculous Crucifix of Esquípulas

PILGRIMAGES INSPIRE A RICH ASSORTMENT OF LEGENDS and folktales, and the Santuario at El Potrero is no exception. Innumerable tales about the miraculous crucifix and the curative powers of the blessed earth associated with it provide the faithful with ample evidence that their religion is very much alive in the Chimayo valley and that God demonstrates His omnipotence through miracles, wonders, and signs.

There is no written record of the origin of the crucifix of Our Lord of Esquípulas, but many versions of how it came to be discovered have been handed down by word of mouth. Cleofas M. Jaramillo, who was raised in Arroyo Hondo, tells one version of the legend:

One morning a mule came down the mountain at Chimayó and stood for hours before the door of the fabled church until someone called the sacristan's attention to it. The man came out to investigate and found that the mule carried across its saddle a long coffin-like box.

On opening the box, they found inside it a small statue of a saint nailed on a cross. The sacristan took the statue and placed it in the Church, giving it the name of Nuestro Señor de Esquípula. Soon the news spread that a miraculous statue had appeared. People from over all the state visited the statue to pay votive promises; some devotees holding lighted candles crawled on their knees to the statue.

For many years, before Don Bernardo Abeyta built the attractive church, wonderful cures had been performed by a strange virtue of the soil taken from a hole in the mud floor. People deformed or suffering with a malady beyond the curative power of physicians flocked to the Santuario, inspired with faith that the Divine Providence, through the supernatural remedial power manifested in the soil and in the miraculous statue, would alleviate their suffering or restore their health. The pilgrims who came from a distance took back with them some of the earth and used it to abate violent storms by throwing a few grains of the earth into a blazing fire. When the smoke reached the top of the chimney, it calmed the storm and changed the course of the lightning (Jaramillo 1941:107-108).

A commonly accepted version comes from a granddaughter of Bernardo Abeyta:

It was during a Holy Week when Bernardo Abeyta, a good member of the fraternity Jesus Nazareno or Penitentes, was performing the customary penances of the society around the hills of Potrero that he suddenly saw a bright light shining from a hole in the ground near the Santa Cruz river. He rushed to the spot and with his bare hands dug out the miraculous crucifix of Our Lord of Esquípulas. He called all the people of El Potrero to see and venerate the precious finding. They soon notified Father Sebastián de Alvarez, and a procession was organized to take the crucifix to Santa Cruz. It was placed in the niche of the main altar. Next morning the crucifix disappeared from its niche and was found again in the same hole where it was first discovered. Another procession was formed to carry it back to Santa Cruz, but the same thing happened this time and once more after it had been taken to Santa Cruz for the third time. By this everyone understood that the crucifix wished to remain in El Potrero, and to venerate it properly, a chapel was built above the hole (Borhegyi 1956:17-18).

In 1925 Juan Abeita of Isleta Pueblo told another version of this legend to anthropologist Elsie Clews Parsons:

One time when a man was out herding sheep he found Escapu'la, a little head sticking out from the ground. He dug this santu out from the ground and carried him all the time on his back while he was herding. He went home. "My wife," he said, "I found this pastor. I am going to keep him. Whenever I go he shall go with me." "All right." They kept him in that little hole. When the man went herding, he carried him on his back again. The santu was right there with him. Then the man went and told the priest that he had found him. The priest told him to carry him to Santa Fe. He carried him there. When he came home, he found him back in his little hole. "Well, come out herding with me," he said to him. The old woman said, "Someday I am going to burn him up." "No!" The man went out herding. On his return he found his wife all crooked, her mouth pulled to one side. He prayed and she prayed, to the santu, to make her look as she did before. So she got well again. So people say that when they make a promise to San Escapu'la they must keep it (Parsons 1932:415-416).

This tale contains a motif similar to the Mayan Indian belief in the malevolent nature of the Black Christ.

Other stories describe the crucifix being found in a hollow tree, near a large rock, or protruding from the earth. Still others describe an apparition of San Esquípulas that leads the witness to the spot of healing dirt. In several versions the finder is cured of an ailment. The name Esquípulas was variously changed to Esquípula, Escapul, Itípula, or Destípula depending on the source. Elements most common to the stories were the sacred object's proximity to the earth, its discovery and disappearance, its return to the original location, and its miraculous healing power.

These naratives fall within a body of legends known as *el ciclo de los pastores*, or "the shepherd's cycle,"[6] that had wide distribution in Europe from the ninth through thirteenth centuries. The legends describe the discovery of images of the Virgin Mary by shepherds, cowherds, and farmers, and although details vary considerably, all exhibit a strikingly uniform thematic structure. The holy images are "found in the ground by knocking a dirt clod aside, in caves while fetching lost sheep, in ponds, in streams, on islands, and in trees." The shepherd is usually led to the discovery by a miraculous happening, such as an unnatural light, the appearance of the Virgin in a vision, or an unexpected noise. Distinctive features of the stories include "mysterious lights, celestial harmonies, demonstrations of adoration and respect by some animals in a rustic and little frequented place, doubts and vacillations by the favored shepherd, attempts to carry the image and worship it privately, incredulity on the part of the people of the town where the miraculous vision is reported, attempts to carry the image to a more comfortable and accessible place, return by the image two or three times to the site of the vision, resolution to build a church in the designated place, and frequent veneration of the image there by people of the town" (Turner 1978:41).

It has been proposed that finding so many objects in the ground resulted from the fact that sacred images were often buried to protect them from being profaned by other religious groups. Since religious objects were often made of silver, the long exposure to nitrates and other chemicals in the soil corroded the metal, turning it black, thus explaining the frequent reference to "Black Virgins" in the medieval stories. Columbus, Cortés, and the *conquistadores* carried replicas of such statues with them on their journeys, and the Franciscan missionaries who were with them spread the veneration in the newly occupied countries, particularly in Mexico (Turner 1978:44).

Buried religious treasure was also a popular folklore theme in Spain dating to the years of Moorish occupation. At the time of New World exploration these tales inspired the *conquistadores* who penetrated the wilderness in search of the Seven Cities of Gold. Variations of the treasure stories of New Spain were based on the old Moorish legends and on actual events in the New World. During the colonial era valuable possessions, including sacred objects, were buried for many reasons: threat of Indian attack, a distrust of banks, eccentricity, or to keep them out of outlaws' hands. The occasional discovery of a cache inspired folktales about great wealth suddenly gained or lost.

New Mexicans from villages like Chimayó believed treasure was protected by supernatural powers, guarded by the elements, or a spirit, and the finder was thought to have somehow allied himself with the Powers. Seasons played a part, for it was believed that during Lent the treasure lay closer to the surface of the ground, and finding wealth hinged on the individual's adhering to traditional values of valor, innocence, and religious conviction (Brown 1978:107; Briggs 1985).

The legends of the miraculous crucifix from Chimayó share several themes with the medieval European legends. First, it is a simple person who finds the crucifix or sees the vision: a farmer, a child, or a shepherd. The shepherd component is related to the story of the birth of Christ (Luke 2:7-20), when shepherds had a vision of the angel of the Lord and went on a "pilgrimage" to witness the "sign," the Christ Child lying in a manger, or, in other versions of the story, in a cave (Turner 1978:42). Second, domesticated animals—sheep, horses, mules—appear in both the medieval stories and those from nineteenth-century Chimayó.[7] Finally, the image of the earth itself, either as a vessel that contains a sacred object or as having healing powers, is a theme that recurs constantly in the legends.

Today, most visitors assume that the large crucifix of Señor Esquípulas behind the Santuario's main altar is the one described in the legends. Nearly six feet high, it is different from the usual *santero* work in that it is painted dark green and decorated with painted gold leaves, iconography stemming from a tradition about how the cross of Esquípulas miraculously sprouted fresh green leaves and branches, symbolizing Christ's power of spiritual regeneration (Wroth 1982:203). The carver of the Chimayó crucifix may have been influenced by engraved images of Our Lord of Esquípulas which were widespread throughout Mexico and produced in quantities for pilgrims to His shrines. Like other images in the small booklets of prayers and the single broadsheets, they tended toward simplicity, ignoring naturalism and maintaining almost Gothic forms centuries after they had been abandoned in other media (Wroth 1982:107).

In the 1950s, Stephen F. de Borhegyi noted another crucifix on the altar, one forty-five centimeters high and in a glass window case. He did not identify it as Señor Esquípulas. However, local people like Chimayó store owner Elma Bal insist that this small crucifix is the one of Our Lord of Esquípulas that was miraculously discovered in the ground. Approximately eighteen inches high, it now stands in a glass window case in the room with the sacred mud.

Whichever crucifix figures in the legends, it is clear that the symbolism is related to the medieval European "shepherd's cycle" narratives and stems from the Christian belief in the birth of Christ and the adoration of the shepherds. It also appears to be related to traditional treasure tales from the Moorish occupation of Spain and the New World variants. On a deeper level, perhaps, the miraculous discovery of the crucifix symbolizes a fundamental belief in resurrection, the "death and burial" of the sacred image and its "restoration to life" by miraculous means.

Santo Niño of the Santuario

The Santo Niño de Atocha

THE REPUTATION OF THE MIRACULOUS CRUCIFIX of Esquípulas which attracted pilgrims to the Chimayó valley brought fame and revenue to Bernardo Abeyta's Santuario. Because miracles had happened in the past and might happen again the pilgrims hoped to be blessed by divine, unseen forces transmitted through the Santuario's various holy images. For nearly half a century, therefore, the crucifix of Esquípulas continued to be revered. But during the mid-1800s a new religious symbol began to supersede it and by the end of the nineteenth century the Mayan-named cult of Esquípulas was no longer associated with the miracles.

The story is that after Abeyta died in 1856 a neighbor of his named Severiano Medina was stricken with severe rheumatism.[8] In his pain he received a revelation instructing him to pray for healing to the Santo Niño de Atocha, whose shrine was in the town of Plateros in the State of Fresnillo in Mexico. Medina prayed, vowing that if he was cured he would make a pilgrimage to the shrine. Recovered from rheumatism he kept his word and in Plateros described his revelation to the priest of the church who, at Medina's request, gave him a statue of the Holy Child of Atocha to take home. He return with it to El Potrero on February 15, 1857, and the people were so delighted by the *santo* that they gave land for the construction of a private chapel to be dedicated to the Santo Niño.[9] A year later the completed chapel was ornamented and permission received to celebrate the Catholic Mass in it.

The new chapel was built about two hundred yards northwest of Abeyta's Santuario and was smaller. (Its dimensions were increased by Ramon Medina in the twentieth century.) Instead of two bell towers like those of the Santuario, a single free-standing campanile was erected to the right of the south entrance.[10]

The first evidence of the hold the cult of the Santo Niño would have on the people of the locality is the 1857 christening of a child, Manuela de Atocha, in Santa Cruz parish, ten miles from El Potrero. The Niño cult took root rapidly and its beliefs soon became blurred with the legends of Esquípulas. Folktales combining old and new began to be told.

It was said that the statue of the Santo Niño had been found in the hole with the healing dirt by a child or a farmer lured to the site by some mysterious phenomenon like the ringing of church bells from underground. Such stories often included the medieval motif of the sacred object's mysterious disappearance and return to the shrine, but less emphasis was placed on the specific location of worship. Instead, the Santo Niño was an image with a life and will of its own; it was said to disappear from its niche, then return with its feet wet and its shoes worn out, a description that best fits into the seventeenth century category of "images that leave their niches, go out of their churches, and walk along the streets and roads, almost as if this were their habit" (Robe 1980:513). Because the Santo Niño wore out his shoes as He wandered about the countryside at night helping those in trouble, pilgrims brought offerings of baby shoes to the chapel and placed them at the feet of the statue, a tradition that continues to this day.[11]

Images of the Santo Niño de Atocha almost always show Him seated, dressed in pilgrim's clothing with a broad brimmed hat, carrying a staff and gourd, and wearing shoes. He also carries a basket generally containing roses and his staff is sometimes decorated with ribbons. Often his ankles are shackled together. Actually the "statue" Severiano Medina brought from Mexico is believed to have been a German papier-mâché doll bent into a sitting position in a wooden chair so that it would resemble the Santo Niño de Atocha (Borhegyi 1956:22).

Few religious figures ever had so strong an appeal to the Hispanics of northern New Mexico. The Child's activities, good or bad, were the common stuff of fireside stories, for to those devout people the spiritual world was as real as the temporal one. By 1864 there was even a small village named El Santo Niño near the old Santa Cruz mission. Generally the sainted Child was considered by the people to be helpful, but now and then he was blamed for destructive events, such as a torrential storm that ruined crops, and called *un mal hijo* (a bad son) (Bullock 1976:62).

As the chapel of El Santo Niño gained popularity the Santuario de Esquípulas lost it. Its owners "in a desperate attempt to rescue the dwindling revenue obtained another Santo Niño figure and announced that in the Santuario, not only the Santo Niño but San Jose, San Rafael, and Santiago also traveled through the country at night and needed new shoes." They too were careless in their choice of a Santo Niño and instead acquired a small wooden *bulto* of the Holy

Child of Prague who carries a globe in His right hand (Borhegyi 1956:22). Further confusion arose when the image was erroneously called the Santo Niño Perdido (The Lost Child), referring to the time when Christ remained in the Temple at the age of twelve and had to be sought by His parents.

Like so many legends of New Mexico and Mexico, it was supposed for many years that the story of the Santo Niño de Atocha could be traced back to Spain during the time of the Moors.

In the city of Atocha, in Spain, many Spanish Christians were imprisoned during the later years of the Moorish occupation. The Moorish conquerors forbade all persons to enter the prison on errands of mercy excepting little children. Not even priests were permitted to bring consolation to the dying. The mothers and wives of these prisoners, knowing that they lacked sufficient food and water, as well as spiritual consolation, prayed daily and passionately for Divine aid in permitting some way of bringing comfort to those in captivity.

One day a child, dressed like the pilgrims of that time, came into the prisons carrying in one hand a basket and, in the other, a staff with a gourd full of water at its tip. To the astonishment of the Moors, the gourd and the basket of bread still were not empty after all of the captives had been served and each one, as he received his portion received also a blessing. According to the legend, Christ had returned in answer to the prayers of the women of Atocha. As a child, He came to serve those without spiritual and earthly help (Boyd 1946:126-127).

E. Boyd's pioneer work has since been expanded by Charles M. Carrillo (unpublished research, University of New Mexico), who has shown that although there is a suburb of Madrid, Spain, called Atocha, there was not a cult of the Santo Niño there at the time it was introduced into Mexico and New Mexico. The name Atocha was probably used very early in the Americas by the Spanish who venerated an image known as the Virgin of Atocha in a church of the Dominican Order of Preachers in Atocha, Spain. The statue was that of a seated Virgin Mary holding the Christ Child on her knee.

In the late 1700s the church of El Santo Cristo de los Plateros in the silver mining area of Fresnillo, Mexico, was given a statue of the Virgin of Atocha brought from Spain by a landowner of the community. At some point in the nineteenth century, possibly when the church burned, the Child was removed from the main statue and venerated independently, thus acquiring the title of Santo Niño de Atocha (Lange 1978:3-7). Carrillo suggests that the Santo Niño cult may have an earlier origin. In pre-Hispanic times the Aztecs worshipped a child-god named Teopiltzintli who was the guardian of travelers and pilgrims. Perhaps Mexican-Indians in colonial Mexico adopted the Santo Niño de Atocha as a surrogate for the child-god who supposedly had led the Aztecs to the site of their sacred homeland, Aztatlen.

The Santo Niño de Atocha became the patron saint of prisoners and travelers in New Mexico as well. Settlers in northern New Mexico were frequently threatened by roving bands of Indians, much as the Christian Spanish had been by the Moors in the Middle Ages. The frequent kidnapping of Spanish children and adults by Indian raiders increased the settlers' devotion to the Holy Child and stories about His rescuing people from captivity were common in New Mexico in the nineteenth and even the twentieth centuries. Cleofas M. Jaramillo of Arroyo Hondo relates one such story:

A mother whose two-year-old son was stolen by Indians during a raid on her town had for years hunted and prayed to find him, but unsuccessfully. Hearing of the miraculous Santo Niño, she promised a novena in honor of the Holy Child. She poured out her grief in her prayers. The last day of the novena came and she had not heard of her child. Frantic with grief, the mother strolled out of the house and followed a road leading to the hills through an arroyo. She had not gone far when she tumbled on an object in the road. Stooping down she picked up the object—a little hat carved out of stone, round-brimmed, with two carved ostrich plumes across the high top.

"A Santo Niño's hat," she was thinking, as she walked along examining the little article. She heard a wagon approaching, and looked up. She saw a man driving, and sitting beside him was a four-year-old boy. Recognizing him as her son, the distracted mother ran up to the wagon, signalling the man to stop.

"My son!" cried the mother, as the child jumped down into her arms. When the happy mother turned to thank the man, both he and the wagon had disappeared. No trace of them could be seen on the road (Jaramillo 1941:108-109).

Pilgrims visited the shrine of the Santo Niño because they had made a vow or *promesa* to the Holy Child for His intercession on behalf of themselves or a loved one. The essence of their pilgrimage was this vow, which said, in effect: "If you, the powerful one, help me in my weakness and affliction, I will later obey you and do what you require of me" (Turner 1978:128).[12] According to Stephen F. de Borhegyi, in 1890 María Martínez, the famed potter of San Ildefonso pueblo, made a pilgrimage to the "Santuario of the Santo Niño" (for by this time the healing power of the earth had been attributed to the Santo Niño). When she was very ill her mother had vowed that if María recovered they would make a pilgrimage to the Santuario to give thanks. "As the little girl rubbed herself with the sacred earth, the mother offered fervent prayers to the Holy Child" (Borhegyi 1956:20-21; also Marriott 1948:39-51).

The Santo Niño cult also reflects an important religious theme deeply rooted in the Judeo-Christian tradition—the potency of the small and weak, illustrated by lines from the Bible such as: "A little child shall lead them" (Isaiah 11:6); "Suffer these little ones to come to me" (Mark 10:11); as well as stories of Christ's infancy and adolescence. Christianity had introduced the concept that the meek and powerless in the world would acquire "sacred power" and thus human littleness became associated with the good of the community as opposed to selfish individual interests. This attitude expanded to include the fertility of man, animals, and crops made possible with an even distribution of power (not too much of anything, just a "little" here and there). Littleness also marks the beginning of the life-cycle, which is often equated with the seasonal cycle (Turner 1978:73-74).

It has been suggested that when the Spanish turned to images of God such as the Trinity, God the Father and the Spirit, and Christ in his Passion, represented in Chimayó by Nuestro Señor de Esquípulas, they were seeking help in the realm of the strictly supernatural, which has to do with faith, charity, holiness, and salvation (Steele 1982:138). The earlier devotion to Esquípulas had possessed a national character in that it was an expression of a real need to find identification with the psyche (soul) of the new land. Hence, the appeal of a supernatural image that insistently returns to the same sacred spot of earth; a miracle with special depth and unique-ness of meaning directly applicable to the settlers in the Chimayó valley. But in the middle of the nineteenth century New Mexicans had firmly established roots in their new homeland. At that point their religious belief took the "form" of the Santo Niño and focused on domestic symbols such as The Holy Family, The Flight to Egypt, the Niño de Atocha, and the Niño Perdido. Family bonds, the safety of travelers, the release of prisoners, and the return of those who had been lost were matters of grave concern to the Spanish settlers and the Santo Niño stood for security and divine assistance in their own homeland.

The Santuario in the Territorial and Early Statehood Years

By THE TIME OF STATEHOOD FOR NEW MEXICO in 1912, Hispanic village life in northern New Mexico was much as it had been since the eighteenth century. In Chimayó, for example, the Plaza del Cerro was still the center of the entire valley. The outside world had hardly penetrated, although occasionally a small circus came, bringing clowns, wirewalkers and tumblers. Gypsies *(las turcas)* also came through, asking residents for food and drink in exchange for fortunes and stories. In late summer neighbors helped one another with harvest, cutting wheat and tying chiles into long *ristras* (strings). Once a year the men of the village went into the hills to gather *amole* (yucca root) for making soap and the women gathered at the *acequia* behind the plaza to wash curtains, bedspreads, furniture coverings and linens. Property was kept up and replastering done yearly. Land remained unfenced and doors unlocked as there was little crime (Larcombe 1983:176-178).

Santuario de Chimayó as it appears today

Virtually everyone earned a living by producing crops on individual parcels of land. The land and climate was suited for growing chiles, small fruits, corn, and vegetables. Some families brought in an outside income from weavings made in the winter months of November through February. Before World War I it was an annual custom for the people of Chimayó to take their surplus chile, fruit and homespun blankets in covered wagons into Colorado's San Luis Valley where the goods were bartered for the beans, potatoes, and wool produced there (Weigle 1975:86-90). This commerce recalls a major event of the nineteenth century, the opening of the Santa Fe Trail in 1821.

With the signing of the Treaty of Córdova on August 24, 1821, Mexico gained independence from Spain and New Mexico became part of the Mexican nation. That ended the Spanish ban on foreign trade, and wagon trains of merchandise began to follow the Santa Fe Trail from Missouri bringing far more goods than had been carried by the old mule trains. Santa Fe soon became the trade center for all northern New Mexico. New Mexican entrepreneurs bought goods from the Americans and sold them in northern Mexican towns (Beck 1962:115). Among the many new items introduced were pictures of saints in tin and glass frames and plaster statues of religious figures, some which had never been venerated in New Mexico. Currier and Ives engravings, lithographs, and oleographs from the United States found a ready market in New Mexico because they were less expensive than the handmade *retablos* (Steele 1982:16).[13]

After Stephen Watts Kearney invaded New Mexico in 1846 and it was declared a territory of the United States in 1850, more and more people of different economic, social and ethnic backgrounds poured into the territory, disrupting the established patterns of Pueblo Indian and

Hispanic societies. Since most newcomers spoke English, the term "Anglo" was generally applied to all groups despite differences in national origin (Jenkins and Schroeder 1974:66).

The sudden increase in population in the latter part of the century was due in large part to the coming of the railroad. The Atchison, Topeka & Santa Fe Railway reached Sante Fe and Albuquerque in 1880. In the late 1800s the Denver and Rio Grande Western Railway began a massive program of expansion. Until 1883 only 337 miles of track ran south of Denver; not long after 1,685 miles of track had been laid through high mountain passes and across the agricultural and mining areas of southern and western Colorado and northern New Mexico (Fox 1983:217). The coming of the railroad to what is now Española brought sewing machines, iron stoves, rice, raisins, canned sardines, and other goods to the small plazas of Chimayó, Córdova, and Truchas, which had never before known such luxuries (Atkins 1978:iv).

Colorful advertisements by the railroad companies to lure settlers extolled the Southwest as a rich land of awe inspiring vistas and sublime mountain ranges. Romantic quotations from poets like Longfellow and Keats were sprinkled liberally through the railroad literature, implying that the beauty and solitude of the west would put complacent urban people in touch with God. Indians and Hispanics were represented as "natural" denizens of a pastoral region who lived close to Nature and reveled in health and pleasure (Fox 1983:217-218).

New Mexico had long been a land of fabulous myths, among them the belief that the region was remarkably free of disease. A 1773 account noted that "no diseases have appeared since the settlement of the Province by Spaniards, which can be said to be peculiar to the climate and country," and travelers were reportedly amazed at the "large number of persons who lived to a great old age..." (Fox 1983:215-216). The railroad exploited such legends to attract thousands suffering from health problems, particularly the respiratory diseases that were a major concern at the turn of the century. Booklets with titles like *Health, Wealth, and Pleasure in Colorado and New Mexico* were published with such attractive descriptions as:

The pure, dry air of the plains and the mountains, rarefied by an elevation of from one to two miles above the sea, and often in high degree electrical, is bracing and exhilarating to the lungs. For asthma it is an almost unfailing specific, as hundreds of persons, confirmed asthmatics before coming to Colorado, but here able to breath with comfort, and the enjoyment of health [soon discovered]... (Fox 1983:218).

This sort of literature appealed tremendously to those who believed illness was directly related to climate, a theory that flourished in the medical community from the 1880s until the turn of the century, when it gave way to the germ theory (Fox 1983:213). Towns like Albuquerque and Santa Fe grew because of the railroad that brought thousands of health-seekers hoping to find cures for tuberculosis, asthma, hay fever, rheumatism, eczema, psoriasis, and even acne. Tuberculosis clinics, hot springs resorts, and sanatoriums flourished during the early decades of the twentieth century and overall, health-seekers accounted for one-fifth to one-half of all immigration to the state between 1870 and 1910 (Fox 1983:217-221).

The trains also brought people dissatisfied with life back east. Artists, writers, and anthropologists came for different reasons but all of them appreciated the unspoiled land of New Mexico and its indigenous Hispanic and Indian peoples whose traditional values seemed to be in refreshing contrast to industrial American life. In the 1920s, disenchanted men and women from urban America were seeking to redefine their identities. The apparent dignity, serenity, and communal solidarity of New Mexican villages seemed to offer a haven. Experimenting with new ways of living and avant-garde artistic styles, the "ethnicity-seekers" of the twenties and thirties left records about the land and people that were a peculiar mixture of "social criticism, romantic generalization, true insight, and personal projection" (Fox 1983:224).

No doubt the complex amalgamation of Indian and Spanish beliefs in Chimayó reflected in the hole of sacred earth, the Catholic folk art and legends, and the picturesque church set against a dramatic landscape of eroded hills and verdant river valley, had a strong visual and psychological appeal for these refugee artists and writers. Perhaps they found an underlying unity beneath all the symbolic diversity. Just as the Penitente rituals drew many curious Anglos, so did the Santuario and its mingled Indian and Hispanic religious legends fascinate these creative intelligentsia.

Many attempted to articulate the attraction of Chimayó. Willa Cather makes several references to it in her famous 1927 novel, *Death Comes for the Archbishop*. Edward S. Curtis, Elsie Clews Parsons, and John Peabody Harrington recorded ethnological accounts. Raymond Jonson painted and drew the landscape around Chimayó,[14] and Ansel Adams took several photographs of the Santuario and its interior.

Of all who wrote about the Southwest and helped express the character by which we know it today, Mary Austin perhaps best symbolizes the spirit of "Anglo" involvement. A strong-willed,

Mary Austin 1929

Interior of the Santuario. Photo by John Boland.

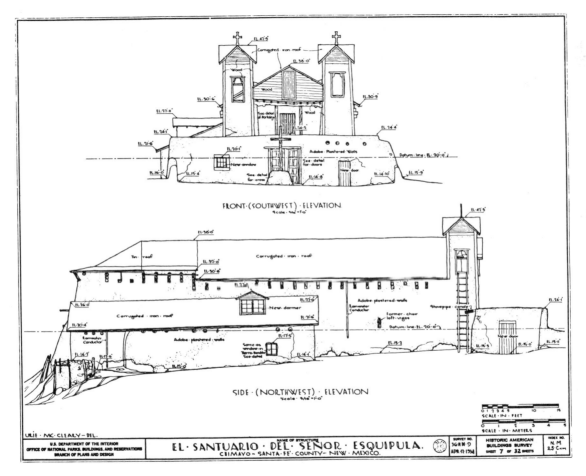

Front and side elevations of El Santuario de Chimayó, from the 1934 Historic American Buildings Survey.

intelligent woman who moved west in 1888, Austin struggled to develop an independent mind and teach herself to write. In 1897 she exchanged her mother's definition of prayer as a fatalistic "acceptance of what life brought" for that of an old Paiute medicine man to whom "prayer was an outgoing act, expressed in dance, words, music, rhythm, color, or whatever medium served the immediate purpose, which acted with the effective principle of the universe with the sureness of a chemical combination" (Austin 1932:276). When Austin met William James in Oakland during one of his lecture tours she discoursed on Paiute spiritual ideas and the possibility that when with the old Indian people she could receive "ancestral experience" (Fox 1983:222).

After living in artistic circles in Carmel and Europe, Austin joined Mabel Dodge's group of artistic friends in New York in 1913 and four years later followed her to New Mexico, where she settled permanently. In the mid-twenties Austin and her Santa Fe neighbor, painter-sculptor Frank G. Applegate, realizing that the handcrafts of New Mexican artisans should be preserved before they disappeared altogether in modern times, revived a society which had first been instituted in 1913 for the preservation of Spanish antiquities. After its incorporation in October of 1929, the new Spanish Colonial Arts Society began to assemble "a permanent collection of the best examples of the old work," offering prizes for blanket weaving, handmade furniture, figure carving, tin work, and other local arts and crafts. The Society also revived the old Spanish drama and organized a theater to preserve the Hispanic verbal heritage as well as the old visual arts (Weigle 1983:183-187). The Santuario was also of concern.

Despite all these efforts to preserve the past, the Chimayó valley had changed greatly since the early years of the twentieth century. The influx of Americans into the Middle Rio Grande

Valley had threatened traditional village systems of subsistence in Chimayó and other small plazas where economic life had always been frugal. The already small parcels of irrigable land were further subdivided and in 1915 new grazing regulations were instituted following the government's consolidation of public lands to national forests. Sheep and cattle permits were reduced and goats excluded entirely from some areas, which diminished livestock production. At the same time a gradual shift from a barter system to a cash economy confronted the villagers with the problem of earning money. For many Hispanics the only recourse was to find summer and spring jobs in other states. It has been estimated that before the Depression some seven to ten thousand workers from villages in the Middle Rio Grande Valley left each year to work in sheep camps or to harvest crops in Colorado, Utah, Wyoming, Montana, and other western states (Brown 1978:13-14; Weigle 1975).

The Santuario had been handed down from one Abeyta family member to another until the 1920s, when it belonged to María de los Angeles Cháves, granddaughter of Bernardo Abeyta, who had inherited it from her mother Carmen Abeyta de Cháves. Financial difficulties owing partly to even fewer pilgrims, forced the Cháves family to begin dismantling the chapel and offering its contents for sale to curio and antique dealers. Not realizing how valuable the old *retablos* and *bultos* were or else under the impression that the Lord would be more pleased with new and inexpensive images, the Cháves family was about to sell the carved wooden doors of the Santuario when Santa Fe artist Gustave Baumann learned of the situation and alerted *Santa Fe New Mexican* editor E. Dana Johnson. Johnson, Frank Applegate, architect John Gaw Meem, and others publicized the chapel's plight.

Lecturing on the East Coast, May Austin was able to persuade an anonymous Yale alumnus to give five thousand dollars toward the eventual purchase price of six thousand dollars. The sum was paid in cash at the owners' home in Chimayó. According to Beatrice Chauvenet:

The deed was dated October 15, 1929, conveying "un capilla titulada el Santuario del Señor Esquípula" to Albert T. Daeger, the Roman Catholic Archbishop of the Archdiocese of Santa Fe, in trust for the Church. It covered only a narrow border of land around the chapel, the sacristy, and the cemetery—ten feet on the east and twelve feet on the west and north, while on the south it was described as bordering the public road. The sellers were José Chavez and Dorotea M. de Chavez, his wife, who retained all the surrounding land. Mrs. Chavez signed by mark, with John Gaw Meem and Paul A. F. Walter witnessing her signature. Victor Ortega and Mareos Chavez signed as witnesses to the transfer (Chauvenet 1985:68).

The deed was later ceremonially handed to Archbishop Daeger in the cathedral garden in Santa Fe. The Santuario was then assigned to Santa Cruz as one of its missions under the care of the priests of the Congregation of the Sons of the Holy Family. In 1970 the shrine was designated as a National Historic Landmark (Weigle 1983:186).

Pilgrimage to Chimayo

EACH YEAR DURING HOLY WEEK over ten thousand people make a pilgrimage to Chimayó to visit the Santuario and take away a bit of the sacred earth. Although some Indians from nearby Pueblos participate in the pilgrimage, they are far outnumbered by Hispanic Catholics. Even fewer Anglos visit, perhaps because they do not realize the religious significance of Holy Week to Hispanic Catholics, perhaps because the concept of sacrifice expressed through pilgrimage is less strongly part of their religious heritage.

Suffering and salvation are the key elements of the traditional pilgrimage to Chimayó, for regardless of distance traversed the journey is made in the spirit of Christ's Passion and underscores the Catholic credo that without suffering there can be no salvation. The walk may vary from over a hundred miles to only a few yards. Genuine suffering can be seen. Some pilgrims are so old or ill they can barely creep over the ground; some are bent under crosses almost too heavy to lift.

Holy Week Pilgrimage

But for many the pilgrimage is much like outings with family or friends, taken in the joy of religious hope and faith. At the end of every pilgrimage comes relief from infinite woes—the Santuario and its pit of healing earth. Thousands claim to have been cured there of diseases, infirmities, and unhappiness. The walls of the sacristy are hung with the evidence of discarded crutches and trusses, with before-and-after photographs.

Pilgrimages are of ancient origin and have been traditional with all the major historical religions—Hinduism, Buddhism, Islam, Judaism, and Christianity. In European societies pilgrimage grew out of a certain set of needs. In medieval Europe the masses were restricted to fixed locales by a rural economy and a feudal political structure that demanded Christian serfs and villiens remain attached to a particular manor or demesnes. Religious worship was physically confined to the local parish and conceptually locked into a doctrine of beliefs. The institution of pilgrimage, though, gave the ordinary man or woman an acceptable justification for leaving family, friends, and the local authorities to visit some distant shrine. Sanctioned by society, pilgrimage became a "complex surrogate for the journey to the source and heartland of the faith" (Turner 1978:4-6). All such journeying symbolized the Way of the Cross, being a sort of penance, beset by hazards, natural dangers, and epidemics. But such perils were fresh and novel, a welcome contrast to the similar evils of home. Furthermore, they were not viewed as the fault of the individual but rather as tests sent by the Almighty (Turner 1978:7).

Leaving familiar scenes behind, the pilgrim entered into a new and deeper level of existence and at the end of the journey was exposed to powerful religious symbols: shrines, images, liturgies, curative substances, and sacralized features of the landscape. The hardship of the journey left

Offerings in the Santuario Sacristy

the pilgrim very vulnerable to such impressions and many have written of the "transformative" effect on them as they reached their destination.

In the 1940s an improved economic climate and the construction of paved roads to Chimayó contributed to a resurgence of pilgrimages to the old shrine. On April 29, 1946, an article appeared in the *Santa Fe New Mexican* newspaper describing a massive pilgrimage to Chimayó:

More than 400, probably the largest congregation ever to attend services in El Santuario, Chimayó's famed chapel, were present at 10 a.m. High Mass yesterday which culminated the weekend pilgrimage of veterans to that tiny community.

Twenty-three veterans—all but two members of New Mexico's 200 coast artillery (AA) which was captured on Bataan—made the 26 mile march, the last 11 miles of which was over mountainous terrain.

At yesterday's service, the pewless, earthen-floored shrine was packed by families of the veterans with an honored place given to those who had lost sons and brothers on Bataan and in Japanese camps.

According to the old custom, the women stood on one side of the church and the men on the other. Santo Niño and other prized statues were in holiday array.

After the service with its sermon in Spanish had been completed, those in the patio surged into the chapel and the little side shrine was crowded with a patient stream of supplicants who gathered handfuls of the soil from the dry well which supposedly has curative powers (La Farge 1959:370-371).

From then on the shrines of Chimayó began to attract tourists and pilgrims. Today thousands visit Chimayó each year.

For many pilgrims the journey to the Santuario is made in an effort to free oneself or a loved one from affliction or to receive the gift of resignation to painful circumstances. Innumerable hopes and woes are involved in mass pilgrimage movements for all have faith that the religion's teachings and symbols will restore order and meaning to a senseless state of affairs.

April in the foothills of northern New Mexico can be cold and despite springtime fruit tree blossoms there is a chance of rain or snow. Yet during the Lenten season, the period marking the forty days preceding the crucifixion of Christ, thousands of pilgrims journey to the Plaza del Potrero with its Santuario and chapel of the Santo Niño. Many who will not visit the village at any other time of the year join the crowds during Holy Week, coming on weekdays or on weekends when schools and jobs are closed. The country roads, ordinarily empty, are congested with cars and people on foot.

The weather plays a major role in the event. In cold wet years few are hardy enough to make a long walk and in these seasons Chimayó shopkeepers may have only a fraction of their usual customers. Good weather, though, may bring up to ten thousand Holy Week visitors. Although the Santuario and its hole of miraculous dirt is their main destination, the walk is still part of the process of redemption and regeneration. Regardless of how far the journey, every pilgrimage is a "sacrifice" undertaken in the spirit of Christ sacrificing Himself to save mankind from sin through the promise of eternal life.

In the early mornings and at noon during Holy Week a priest from Santa Cruz conducts Mass. Late in the afternoon he may take a group of worshippers behind the Santuario to an outdoor shrine within a cottonwood grove by the Santa Cruz river. Stopping briefly at each

A Chimayó Pilgrim

Station of the Cross, the priest reads liturgy. The Stations symbolize the humiliation and agony suffered by Christ, and the pilgrims, following a credo taught for generations, feel that only by experiencing similar torment can they hope to find their way to Salvation.

A pilgrimage begins when an individual makes a vow to God or the saints that he or she will walk if they or someone they care about is freed from present trouble (Turner 1978:13). An example of this kind of promise was a man from Grants, New Mexico, who carried a 6-foot cross 137 miles to Chimayó when his son returned unharmed from Vietnam. Others walk in hope that the act of faith and the sacred dirt will cure them or someone they care for from illness. Distances of well over a hundred miles have been covered by pilgrims on foot according to testimonials in the Santuario.

Most start walking at Santa Fe, twenty-seven miles away, but it is not uncommon for pilgrims to walk the eighty miles from Albuquerque. Some walk part of the way barefoot or crawl the last few yards on their knees, a common tradition in Spain and Latin America. Those who wish to walk but are physically incapable are dropped off near the shrine by friends or family who will later drive them home. Still others come on horseback or jog.

Certainly the physical hardship of the walk and the barrage of visual symbols such as crosses, shrines, and holy objects encountered on the journey must shift the mental balance and intensify the experience of the pilgrim. Religious images may strike the individual as never before, even though they may be very familiar objects seen almost daily. In such a mental state the pilgrim may feel he or she has had some personal confrontation with spiritual forces.

A strong sense of fellowship arises among the pilgrims on the road, and to be part of hundreds of people all walking together toward a shared goal is a heady sensation. The arid, eroded New Mexican landscape of mesas, arroyos, and distant mountains adds to the spell. Pilgrims from the south who enter the irrigated Nambe valley between the pueblos of Pojoaque and Tesuque see a countryside of cultivated fruit orchards but soon climb out of it as the road winds up weathered sandstone and scrub-covered hills to the overwhelming view of sky and land that dwarfs human beings. In this desolate land families gather along the road to give coffee to the pilgrims as their contribution to the ritual. They will not go into Chimayó; this is their offering, miles from the shrine.

Five miles from Chimayó solitary crosses begin to dot the hills, marking the pilgrim's way and indicating that the central shrine is near. At the foot of some crosses stones have been heaped by pilgrims who stopped to pray before going on. Other crosses stand on the tops of hills too steep for most to climb, although their sites offer sweeping views of the landscape. These crosses are the first of many symbolic forms a pilgrim meets which help him become "capable of entering in imagination and with sympathy into the culturally defined experience of the founder and of those persons depicted as standing in some close relationship to him, whether it be of love or hate, loyalty or awe." They also serve to slow the pilgrim's progress so as to build up a reservoir of reverent feeling that will brim over in a climactic flood when the final shrine is reached (Turner 1978:10-11, 23).

As the road descends from the desolate countryside into the Chimayó valley where the trees are just beginning to leaf out, the mood of the pilgrim is sober. The goal is near and all the senses are concentrated on it. People on foot, cars, and grazing cattle along the roadside slow

Shrine South of Chimayó

progress. At the entrance to the plaza police direct the chaotic flow of traffic.

The plaza teems with hundreds of people, many waiting patiently to enter the Santuario, others strolling into nearby stores which sell food, film, and religious articles. These stores are also "sacred aspects" of the pilgrimage, as are markets, hospices, hospitals, military supports, legal devices, systems of communication and transportation which combine in the environment "field" (Turner 1978:22). All available benches and walls are taken by weary people resting from their walk and watching the crowd. Their clothing indicates they come from vastly different economic backgrounds and yet pilgrimage is a great leveler, illustrated by the commonness of purpose shared by the variegated crowd.

Good Friday was traditionally a time in Hispanic villages when Tenebrae services for the dead were held. Within this tradition pilgrims in the Santuario pray for those who have passed away. Others do not stop in the nave but slowly make their way to the tiny anteroom where they scoop some earth from the hole in the floor before exiting through a door in the rear of the sacristy. Having reached the destination of the most holy of shrines the pilgrim carries back, and to some extent is in possession of, sacred power. Although priests periodically refill the hole with dirt from outside the church, legend still maintains that the hole miraculously replenishes itself.

Once the ritual of taking away sacred dirt is accomplished, the pilgrims visit the chapel of the Santo Niño de Atocha or climb a nearby hill to the tiny private chapel of San Antonio before returning home. The mood of the return trip is much different. Having done penance, paid devotion, and achieved an emotional climax at the center of the shrine, the pilgrim is now ready to relax and return home as quickly as possible. Most drive home, although a devout few may walk.

The pilgrim has not changed his or her social status by the journey, but they know they have made a spiritual step forward. Roman Catholicism has conceived the process of salvation as a lifelong drama of the individual human soul and thus pilgrimage is regarded as "good work."

Epilogue

TRADITIONAL PILGRIMAGE AS DESCRIBED ABOVE is not the only kind that centers around the old shrine. On April 14, 1984, the Santuario de Chimayó was the scene of a modern pilgrimage. Over 450 people gathered in the cottonwood grove behind the church for a mass celebrated by Archbishop Robert Sanchez, the leader of the Santa Fe Archdiocese, who explained that the gathering was a "prayer pilgrimage for peace" begun in "a place made holy by the love and sacrifice of many people" who have sought its healing soil.[15]

A small bag of earth from the Santuario was blessed by the Archbishop and following the celebration of Holy communion, the bag was handed to fifteen runners who carried the soil in different relays to Ashley Pond in Los Alamos. Behind the runners pilgrims walked three miles to Holy Family Church in Chimayó and, after driving to Los Alamos, walked another two miles to Ashley Pond where floated a "Raft of Life" filled with homemade breads, tulips, apple blossoms,

Peace Pilgrimage to Chimayó, 1985. Photo by Ray Bal.

Peace Pilgrimage to Chimayó, 1985. Photo by Ray Bal.

forsythia, juniper branches, balloons, and blankets.

Thus, modern pilgrimage has become a critique of problems that plague modern people in the predominant social structure. "Its emphasis on transcendental, rather than mundane, ends and means; its generation of communitas; its search for roots of ancient, almost vanished virtues as the underpinning of social life" have contributed to a dramatic resurgence of pilgrimage in recent years (Turner 1978:38).

Chimayó can be described as a "cultural magnet," attracting symbols of many kinds to which we cannot help but respond in some way, being as we are, creatures that create symbols as a means of comprehending and even celebrating the ambiguities, puzzles and paradoxes of life. Acting as a channel between our reason and emotion, between the rational and nonrational in the human psyche, the many symbols contained in and around the Santuario de Chimayó are messages of protection and security, of healing and regeneration. They offer hope and comfort to those seeking solutions to the personal and social problems that have always troubled people.

Notes

1. "*Tsimajo* ...[means] 'flaking stone of superior quality' 'town of the flaking stone of superior quality' (*tsi'i* 'flaking stone' of any varient; *majo* 'superior' 'chief' ") (Harrington 1916:314).

2. According to Borhegyi (1953,1954) there are three major opinions concerning the etymology of the word Esquípulas. The most acceptable is that Esquípulas is a Chorti Indian term originally pronounced *Es-kip-ur-ha*. *Kipurha* means "raised water" or spring, probably referring to the sulphurous springs in the area. The *Es* prefix was probably the usual Spanish prefix added to make the word more easily pronounced. Another interpretation is that Esquípulas means "the place where the flowers are abundant." *Isquitl* or *isquitzuchil* is "flower" in the Nahuatl language. *Pal* and *la* are suffixes indicating abundance. Another possibility is that the word *ysquipulas*, meaning "banana tree," was the root.

3. There are variations of the spelling of Abeyta: Beytia and Veitia, for example. The Abeytas were in the campaigns with de Vargas and later acquired land around Santa Fe and the community of Puebla near Santa Cruz. In 1797 Bernardo Abeyta of Pueblo married Rita Valerio of El Potrero and went there to live. The Valerio family had settle in Potrero prior to 1741 (Borhegyi 1956:11).

4. A *retablo* is a painting made on a pine panel, covered with gesso, and painted with homemade watercolors. A *reredo* is a large structure of pine columns, niches, and panels placed behind an altar. A *bulto* is a statue assembled from a carved cottonwood root, covered with gesso, and painted like a *retablo*.

5. Today the church has five *reredos*. One is behind the main altar and two are on each side of the nave. The largest images behind the altar as well as one on the right of the nave were painted by Molleno,

nicknamed the "Chili Painter." It is thought that another *reredo* on the right was painted by Miguel Aragon. The two remaining paintings on the left were done by José Aragon, who lived in nearby Córdova. These three *santeros* produced most of their works between 1820 and 1850.

6. Originally described by Vincent de la Fuente in 1879 in his history of the Spanish cult of Mary (Turner 1978:41).

7. One opinion is that when associated with the Virgin these animal references not only symbolize the beasts present at the Nativity but may also be a link to an earlier Mediterranean cult of the Great Goddess or Earth Mother who was concerned with the fertility of animals, both tame and wild (Turner 1978:42).

8. The story of the Medina chapel comes from an article in the *Santa Fe New Mexican* newspaper dated March 18, 1979.

9. Private family chapels were traditional in New Mexico from Colonial times. Between 1800 and 1850 forty new chapels were licensed and built in Spanish villages, indicating the population growth at that time (Steele 1983:301).

10. Other opinions are that Medina built his chapel in order to capitalize on the income generated by the pilgrimage (Borhegyi 1956:21).

11. Folktales of the Virgin sometimes describe this same wanderlust. Evidence of her travels appeared in the dust on her gown, the mud on the hem of her skirt, the prints of her bare feet, and the testimony of the faithful who claimed to have seen her on her travels (Robe 1980:513).

12. "It has been suggested that Latin European and Latin American pilgrimages to the shrines of miracleworking images of Christ, the Virgin, or a saint, have the function of maintaining an important aspect of the social structure, that is the relationship between patron and client, which exists both in the quasifeudal property relationship between landowner and peon and in the economic relationship be-

tween merchant and farmer" (Turner 1978:128).

13. Some of the most powerful New Mexican *bultos* date from the period between the peak of the Santa Fe Trail trade and the arrival of the railroad which brought boxcars of statues too heavy to come by wagon train from St. Louis at a profit. The later *bultos* leaned heavily toward raw literalness. Representations of a suffering Christ included real hair and teeth, porcelain eyes, moveable limbs, and realistic description of wounds (Steele 1982:16-18).

14. Jonson's painting "Earth Rhythms #6" (1925) was based on formations near Chimayo. In the painting the forms are easily recognized as earth erosion, sky, etc., but the means used are adapted to a certain concept of color, movement, space, light, and dark in an attempt to convey an underlying sense of order, what Jonson called "a unifying principle" that applies not only to a way of painting but also to a way of living (Garman 1976:51, 56).

15. From an article in the *Albuquerque Journal* dated April 15, 1984.

Bibliography

Atkins, Carolyn
  1978   Los Tres Campos—The Three Fields. Albuquerque, New Mexico: Menaul Historical Library of the Southwest.
Austin, Mary
  1932   Earth Horizon: Autobiography. Cambridge, Massachusetts: Riverside Press.

Beck, Warren A.
  1962   New Mexico: A History of Four Centuries. Norman: University of Oklahoma Press.
Borhegyi, Stephen F. de
  1953   The Miraculous Shrines of Our Lord of Esquípulas in Guatemala and Chimayó, New Mexico. El Palacio 60:83-111. (Reprinted in Borhegyi 1956.)
  1954   The Cult of Our Lord of Esquípulas in Middle America and New Mexico. El Palacio 61:387-401.

  1956   El Santuario de Chimayó. Santa Fe, New Mexico: Ancient City Press for the Spanish Colonial Arts Society.
Boyd, E.
  1946   Saints & Saint Makers of New Mexico. Santa Fe, New Mexico: Laboratory of Anthropology.
Briggs, Charles L.
  1983   A Conversation with Saint Isidore: The Teachings of the Elders. In Hispanic Arts and Ethnohistory in the Southwest, Marta Weigle et al. eds. Pp. 103-15. Santa Fe: Ancient City Press; Albuquerque: University of New Mexico Press.
  1985   Treasure Tales and Pedagogical Discourse in Mexicano New Mexico. Journal of American Folklore 98:287-314.
Brown, Lorin W., with Briggs, Charles L., and Weigle, Marta

1978 Hispano Folklife of New Mexico: The Lorin W. Brown Federal Writers' Project Manuscripts. Albuquerque: University of New Mexico Press.

Bullock, Alice
1976 The Legend of the Santo Niño. New Mexico Magazine, December, pp. 53, 62-63.

Chauvenet, Beatrice
1985 John Gaw Meem: Pioneer in Historic Preservation. Santa Fe: Historic Santa Fe Foundation/Museum of New Mexico Press.

Chavez, Fray Angelico
1974 My Penitente Land. Albuquerque: University of New Mexico Press.

Christiansen, Paige W., and Kottlowski, Frank E.
1967 Mosaic of New Mexico's Scenery, Rocks, and History: A Brief Guide. Socorro: State Bureau of Mines and Mineral Resources, New Mexico Institute of Mining and Technology.

Córdova, Lorenzo de
1972 Echoes of the Flute. Santa Fe, New Mexico: Ancient City Press.

Curtis, Edward S.
1926 The North American Indian. Vol. 17. Norwood, Massachusetts: Plimpton Press.

Darley, Alexander M.
1893 The Passionists of the Southwest, or The Holy Brotherhood: A Revelation of the "Penitentes." Rpt. Glorieta, New Mexico: Rio Grande Press, 1968.

DeHuff, Elizabeth Willis
1931 The Santuario at Chimayo. New Mexico Magazine, June, pp. 16-17.

Eliade, Mircea
1958 Patterns in Comparative Religion. New York: Sheed and Ward.

Fergusson, Erna
1937 Guatemala. New York: Alfred A. Knopf.

Fox, Stephen D.
1983 Healing, Imagination, and New Mexico. New Mexico Historical Review 58:214-37.

Garman, Ed
1976 The Art of Raymond Jonson: Painter. Albuquerque: University of New Mexico Press.

Harrington, John Peabody
1916 Ethnography of the Tewa Indians. *In* Bureau of American Ethnology 29th Annual Report. Pp. 69-342. Washington: GPO.

Henderson, Alice Corbin
1937 Brothers of Light: The Penitentes of the Southwest. New York: Harcourt, Brace.

Jaramillo, Cleofas M.
1941 Shadows of the Past (Sombras del pasado). Santa Fe, New Mexico: Seton Village Press. (Rpt. Ancient City Press, 1980.)

Jenkins, Myra Ellen, and Schroeder, Albert H.
1974 A Brief History of New Mexico. Albuquerque: University of New Mexico Press.

Jones, Oakah L., Jr.
1978 Los Paisanos: Spanish Settlers on the Northern Frontier of New Spain. Norman: University of Oklahoma Press.

Kubler, George
1940 The Religious Architecture of New Mexico: In the Colonial Period and Since the American Occupation. Colorado Springs, Colorado: Taylor Museum.

La Farge, Oliver
1959 Santa Fe: The Autobiography of a Southwestern Town. Norman: University of Oklahoma Press.

Lange, Yvonne
1978 Santo Niño de Atocha: A Mexican
Cult Is Transplanted to Spain. El
Palacio 84, 4: 2-7.

Larcombe, Samuel
1983 Plaza del Cerro, Chimayo, New
Mexico: An Old Place Not Quite on
the Highway. In Hispanic Arts and
Ethnohistory in the Southwest, Marta
Weigle et al. eds. Pp. 171-80. Santa Fe:
Ancient City Press; Albuquerque:
University of New Mexico Press.

Marriott, Alice
1948 Maria: The Potter of San Ildefonso.
Norman: University of Oklahoma
Press.

Ortiz, Alfonso
1969 The Tewa World: Space, Time, Being,
and Becoming in a Pueblo Society.
Chicago: University of Chicago Press.
1979 San Juan Pueblo. In Handbook of
North American Indians, Vol. 9,
Alfonso Ortiz, ed. Pp. 278-94.
Washington, D.C.: Smithsonian Institution Press.

Parsons, Elsie Clews
1932 Isleta, New Mexico. Bureau of
American Ethnology 47th Annual
Report. Rpt. Albuquerque: Calvin
Horn Publisher, 1974.
1939 Peublo Indian Religion. Vol. 1.
Chicago: University of Chicago Press.

Robe, Stanley L.
1980 (Ed.) Hispanic Legends from New
Mexico: Narratives from the R.D.
Jameson Collection. Folklore and
Mythology Series: 31. Berkeley:
University of California Press.

Simmons, Marc
1966 New Mexico's Smallpox Epidemic of
1780-1781. New Mexico Historical
Review 41:319-26.

1983a Carros y Carretas: Vehicular Traffic on the Camino Real. *In* Hispanic Arts and Ethnohistory in the Southwest, Marta Weigle et al. eds. Pp. 325-34. Santa Fe: Ancient City Press; Albuquerque: University of New Mexico Press.

1983b Colonial New Mexico and Mexico: The Historical Relationship. *In* Colonial Frontiers: Art and Life in Spanish New Mexico, The Fred Harvey Collection, Christine Mather, ed. Pp. 71-89. Santa Fe: Ancient City Press.

Steele, Thomas J., S.J.

1982 Santos and Saints: The Religious Folk Art of Hispanic New Mexico. Santa Fe: Ancient City Press.

1983 Naming of Places in Spanish New Mexico. *In* Hispanic Arts and Ethnohistory in the Southwest, Marta Weigle et al. eds. Pp. 293-302. Santa Fe: Ancient City Press; Albuquerque: University of New Mexico Press.

Steele, Thomas J., S.J., and Rivera, Rowena

1985 Penitente Self-Government: Brotherhoods and Councils, 1797-1947. Santa Fe: Ancient City Press.

Turner, Victor and Edith

1978 Image and Pilgrimage in Christian Culture: Anthropological Perspectives. New York: Columbia University Press.

Walter, Paul A. F.

1916 A New Mexico Lourdes. El Palacio 3, 2: 3-27.

Weigle, Marta

1970 The Penitentes of the Southwest. Santa Fe: Ancient City Press.

1975 (Ed.) Hispanic Villages of Northern New Mexico: A Reprint of Volume II of The 1935 Tewa Basin Study, with Supplementary Materials. Santa Fe, New Mexico: The Lightning Tree.

1976 Brothers of Light, Brothers of Blood: The Penitentes of the Southwest.

Albuquerque: University of New
Mexico Press.

1983　The First Twenty-Five Years of the
Spanish Colonial Arts Society. *In*
Historic Arts and Ethnohistory in the
Southwest, Marta Weigle et al. eds.
Pp. 181-203. Santa Fe: Ancient City
Press; Albuquerque: University of New
Mexico Press.

Wroth, William

1979　The Chapel of Our Lady of Talpa.
Colorado Springs, Colorado: The
Taylor Museum of the Colorado
Springs Fine Arts Center.

1982　Christian Images in Hispanic New
Mexico: The Taylor Museum Collec-
tion of Santos. Colorado Springs,
Colorado: The Taylor Museum of the
Colorado Springs Fine Arts Center.